Little Books of Leadership

Also in the series:

Communication
Crisis Leadership by Margaret Benefiel

RESILIENCE

A little
book of
leadership

CHURCH
PUBLISHING
INCORPORATED

Unless otherwise noted, the Scripture quotations contained herein are from the New Revised Standard Version Bible, copyright © 1989 by the Division of Christian Education of the National Council of Churches of Christ in the U.S.A. Used by permission. All rights reserved.

This book compiles text from the following sources:
Alice Updike Scannell, *Building Resilience: When There's No Going Back to the Way Things Were* (New York: Morehouse Publishing, 2020); Kay Collier McLaughlin, *Becoming the Transformative Church: Beyond Sacred Cows, Fantasies, and Fears* (New York: Morehouse Publishing, 2013); Stephanie Spellers, *Radical Welcome: Embracing God, The Other, and the Spirit of Transformation* (New York: Church Publishing, 2006).

Church Publishing
19 East 34th Street
New York, NY 10016
www.churchpublishing.org

Cover design by Jennifer Kopec, 2Pug Design
Typeset by Progressive Publishing Services

A record of this book is available from the Library of Congress.

ISBN-13: 978-1-64065-406-8 (pbk.)
ISBN-13: 978-1-64065-405-1 (eBook)

Contents

A Word about the
Little Books of Leadership

The deepest roots of the word lead mean "to travel." Other meanings in the word have to do with guiding, showing the way, and conducting, all of which carry a sense of movement: we are on our way to somewhere or something.

In the church setting, that sense of movement lives in creative tension with the institution and the pull of self-preservation. We are people with a deep history and a compelling present tense; we are also a people with a complicated past and an uncertain future. We are always looking for a leader—someone who helps us navigate the journey.

The models of leadership in our present society are myriad. The ones that get the most attention have too often been those that are more directive than collaborative, more authoritarian than inclusive. If we listen closely, we can hear what the apostle Paul called "a gong or a clanging symbol." Leadership that is not based in love rings hollow.

The Little Books of Leadership are an ongoing series designed to offer points of contact and conversation to congregations as they live out the daily journey of what it means to be God's beloved community. To say there is no one-size-fits-all approach is to state the obvious, yet we can learn from one another's stories of what has been done and left undone. We can listen for new rhythms of the Spirit and change how we conduct ourselves in our life together. Jesus said those who wished to lead had to learn how to serve if they were going to be effective, which is to say we are called to attend to one another and respond accordingly. To lead in such a fashion is, to borrow a favorite Episcopal phrase, to travel the Way of Love.

Come, let us travel together.

1 ▪ Defining Resilience

Resilience is the human capacity to live through things: to experience adversity, failure, or other traumatic events, and then live beyond them. It is doing the difficult work of repunctuating life and putting a comma or a semicolon where it feels like life has come to a full stop. Resilience is not just a quality leaders have that enables them to cope with disruptive changes and adapt; it is also their capacity to cultivate the same spirit in their congregations. As researchers from the Seattle School of Theology note:

> Another name for it might be "resurrection."
>
> Jesus's experience leading up to and on the cross is perhaps the epitome of traumatic events. He experiences betrayal from his disciple, condemnation from his religious leaders, brutality at the hands of the government authorities. He is sexually humiliated, physically abused, and spiritually forsaken; then he dies.
>
> Days later, he resurrects. When he first sees the disciples, he says "peace be with you" and shows them his wounds. Through Jeremiah, God condemns prophets and priests who "dress the wounds of my people as though it were not serious. 'Peace, peace, they say, when there is no peace.'" We would expect that Jesus, who has just suffered the trauma of his own death, might know that there is no peace—and yet that's exactly the benediction he opens with.
>
> The resurrected Christ models truth about wounds and peace. He shows, without shame, the wounds of the worst

1

thing that ever happened to him. He allows the meaning of the wounds to be manifest in his resurrected life: that transformation can happen after trauma, that wounds do not preclude new life, that resurrection is the way to resilience.

Far from being an insufficient dressing on a serious wound, when Christ says "Peace be with you," it is an offering of the possibility of peace even after having been wounded. Post-traumatic growth, the coexistence of peace and woundedness, requires the flexibility to develop new resilience skills—coping strategies—through the new challenges we face.

As children and adolescents, people find ways to cope with difficulties through whatever means they can; those coping strategies help people to survive that context. But sometimes the context changes and the coping strategies don't, undermining our ability to thrive. We need flexibility to allow meaning to come from our hardships, to listen to our pasts, and to be open to where God is leading us into the future.[1]

We usually think of resilience as the ability to recover from an adverse experience and pick up our lives where we left off. It is that, but there are times when adversity permanently changes our

---

1. The Resilient Leaders Project. The Seattle School of Theology & Psychology. Report 1: Resilience. http://theseattleschool.edu /wp-content/uploads/2019/02/RLP_Report01_Resilience_Final _web.pdf.

reality and we can't go back to the way things were. We can't do the things we used to do that were part of our identity—the things that gave meaning and purpose to our lives, that gave us a reason to live. It feels as though our quality of life has been smashed to pieces and is gone forever. Fear for our future wrenches our insides. We don't know what we'll do.

When adversity permanently changes our reality, there is no going back to the way things were. Resilience then becomes the work of coming through the adversity so that, at least on most days, we see our life as still worth living. With this kind of resilience, we come through the adversity knowing that we're still ourselves, even though things are very different for us now.

Such resilience is a challenge because it connects with the roots of our being. It draws from our essential self, demanding that we engage with meaning and hope in new ways in order to feel that our life is still worth living. It is also accompanied, at some point, by a surprising sense of gratitude. It is radical because it transforms us, both inwardly and outwardly. We learn that wholeness is a state of being, that life can have meaning and purpose under many different circumstances.

Though our list is not exhaustive, we will look at the following resilience "skills": reframing our reality, encouraging creativity, looking for strengths, fostering compassion, facing our fear, and practicing resurrection.

We call them skills because it takes awareness, intentionality, and practice to develop them. Other people might call them practices or attitudes, but skills implies that we get better at them as we apply them. Alone or in combination, these skills, when used intentionally to respond to any kind of change, open up the path to resilience by helping us to see and do things differently.

Whenever we are challenged by change, we can intentionally practice a resilience skill. As we learn how each of the skills can strengthen our capacity for resilience, we'll become aware of abundant opportunities to practice the skills that hone our capacity to be resilient. These skills help enormously to move us out from a place of despair, frustration, and loss into a more fruitful place of centeredness and inner strength. They help us let go of the past. Moreover, they help us move forward, with hope and a sense of self, into the future. We don't just stumble into resilience, however. We have to prepare ourselves by fostering self-awareness, supportive relationships, openness, reflection, and humor.

Self-Awareness

In order to respond with resilience to changes in our lives and our communities, we must be able to face the truths (both positive and negative) about ourselves and see ourselves as others see us, which includes awareness of our attitudes that are judgmental or biased, of how we communicate with others, and of how well we listen. It also includes the awareness of experiences in our lives that might influence how we interpret situations, how we behave in response to confrontation or criticism, how we view people who are different from us, and how we handle disappointment and loss. All of these, unless acknowledged and understood, may limit our capacity for resilience.

The work of self-awareness applies to both individuals and communities. A congregation that cultivates direct and open communication, avoids anonymous feedback, and makes a point of seeking out the softer voices is setting itself up for resilience because it has a truer picture of who it is. Communal self-awareness included a healthy look at the origin story of the congregation (or denomination), an honest assessment of how it deals with conflict, and an ongoing conversation about hopes and dreams.

Supportive Relationships

It's hard to do the work of resilience alone. Whatever the circumstances of our adversity, we'll do much better if we have people to whom we can talk, with whom we can share our thoughts, and from whom we can request specific assistance or support. Sometimes the people who serve in those roles are not our closest friends or family members. Often they are professionals who have specific training to help us come through our adversity. Or they may be organizations and support groups specifically formed to help people who have experienced similar adversities. It's important to avoid isolation and to find acceptance through a group or a trusted confidante. Having at least one trusted person with whom we can share our deepest concerns and with whom we can be completely honest is central to our sense of well-being not only when we're recovering from adversity but also throughout our life.

The congregational setting is relational by definition. Looking at how the intended structure fosters supportive relationships is crucial work that goes beyond pastoral care and funeral food. A resilient church is one that cultivates connectedness.

Openness

To be open is to be willing to hear honest feedback from people we trust. However, openness also includes being willing to express our thoughts, feelings, doubts, fears, and truths to those people or others we trust. Sharing the stories we're ashamed to tell about ourselves with those who will accept us as we are, respect our stories, and hold our stories in confidence liberates us from the bonds of secrecy and embarrassment. The work of the church is to create relationships that foster the telling of and listening to those seminal stories.

Reflection

Life together requires of us to think about our experiences and learn from them. Reflection is not simply going over and over an experience in our minds. Rather, it is contemplating the experience in order to gain insight. Reflection includes naming the emotions we felt before, during, and after the experience, and asking ourselves what the experience has to teach us. Sometimes reflecting on a current experience will call to mind an experience from the past that links to it, leading us to a deeper understanding of ourselves and how we process some of the things that happen to us. Insights that result from reflection broaden our awareness not only of ourselves but also of possibilities, and they help us to see multiple ways that we can understand or do things differently.

Humor

A gentle sense of humor and an ability to take ourselves lightly when we are stressed increase our capacity for resilience. Both gentle laughter and spontaneous guffaws help dissolve inner tension. They help us relax, and that in itself can give us a refreshed perspective on life. Though many a church meeting is important, or even crucial, keeping a sense of humor reminds us that rarely is anything eternal on the table. Regardless of the meeting or the issue, what matters most are the people involved. Keeping a sense of humor allows us to remember nothing matters more than each other.

2 ▪ Reframing Our Reality

The work of Marilee Adams speaks to the importance of paying attention to our mind-set when we're trying to reframe a situation. Adams has developed a process that she calls Question Thinking,™[2] which is a way of using questions to direct our thinking when we're faced with a problem, a change, or a challenge and we're stuck in negative thoughts and emotions. The Question Thinking process begins with identifying our mind-set.

Adams identifies the mind-sets that we use when dealing with problems, changes, and challenges as the Judger mind-set and the Learner mind-set. The Judger is not about judgment; it's about being judgmental. It is a reaction mind-set. When we're in Judger mind-set, we want to defend ourselves and blame others. We make judgmental statements and ask closed-ended questions that cut off the possibility for raising other perspectives on the issue. Some examples of Judger mind-set thinking are as follows:

> "Whose fault is it?"
>
> "What's wrong with them?"
>
> "How could you do such a thing?"
>
> "That's ridiculous."

---

2. M. Adams, *Change Your Questions, Change Your Life: 10 Powerful Tools for Life and Work*, 2nd ed. (San Francisco, CA: Berrett-Koeler, 2009).

Judger mind-set thinking can also be self-directed: "What's wrong with me?" "Why am I such a failure?" and "I'm so stupid!" The Judger mind-set drains our energy and closes off our capacity for creative thinking.

The Learner is an inquiry mind-set. When we're in Learner mind-set, we are open to learning more about ourselves, as well as inviting other people's perspectives on the situation. Some examples of Learner mind-set thinking are

> "What assumptions am I making?"
>
> "What are my choices?"
>
> "What is the other person feeling, needing, or wanting?"
>
> "What can I learn from this?"
>
> "What other ways can I look at this?"

The Learner mind-set opens us to creative thinking and thus leads to successful reframing. Question Thinking expands the concept of reframing and makes it a powerful resilience skill.

The purpose of reframing is not to ignore reality or engage in unrealistic fantasy. Reframing means that we engage our imaginations in generating a number of different ways we might interpret or understand our situation or experience. Some of the possibilities we imagine may seem so preposterous they make us laugh, but that's good. Laughter relaxes us and eases tension.

The right frame will be the one that changes the way we see our situation so that we feel "unstuck" and can move forward. If we still feel stuck after a session of reframing, we give ourselves a break and try again later. The process itself will most likely have opened our minds, imaginations, and hearts to new perspectives on the challenges that we face.

An oft-repeated maxim is that the seven last words of the church are "We've never done it that way before." Another is that the Japanese symbol for crisis is made up of the symbols for danger and opportunity. Reframing our reality is not a matter of mere semantics, but an understanding that words matter a great deal. How we choose to name things affects how we see them.

Our experiences of congregational life during the pandemic have given us a stronger grasp of reframing because we have had to choose almost daily between focusing on what has been lost and what we are finding in our new ways of being.

A new frame may not change the picture, but it changes how we look at it, which means it opens our hearts to hear the Spirit say, "Behold, I am doing a new thing."

3 ▪ Encouraging Creativity

We draw on our natural creativity many times in our lives without realizing it because creativity is a multifaceted skill that encompasses all the ways we use our imagination to see new ways to solve problems, do tasks, think new thoughts, understand new meanings, find a new use for something, or make something new. Creativity is much more than artistic ability—it is also the ability to think of more than one possibility in response to a given idea, situation, or challenge. Creativity can be expressed through the sciences and technology as well as through the arts. In fact, creativity can be expressed in multiple ways in our daily lives. We expressed our creativity when we were children learning to live in a new, unfamiliar, exciting, and sometimes threatening world. We'd make up songs and stories, thrill to the sensation of making mud pies and later of working with clay. We'd build structures with blocks or Legos and then knock them down so we could put those pieces together a different way. We'd dress up in costumes, dance to music, create tunes on a keyboard, and make colorful pictures of the things in our world that we loved. We expressed joy and sadness, boldness and inquisitiveness, freedom, pleasure, and many other aspects of our inner thoughts and feelings through our creative activity. Expressing ourselves through our creativity helped us—and continues to help us—become who we are.

There's an element of play in creativity that loosens us up and energizes us. Being relaxed from play helps us be attuned to new ideas, new images, new directions, and a new sense of self. Play is called recreation for a reason: it re-creates us. That spark of re-creation ignites our capacity for resilience and provides the energy to go forward.

"Creativity," writes Gene Cohen, "is a process or an outlook, not a product. It is a distinctly human quality that exists independent of age and time, reflecting a deeper dimension of energy capable of transforming our lives at any age."[3]

Creativity includes the ability to imagine connections between disparate objects. This kind of creativity often comes as we're playing around with ideas or observations and a creative connection jumps out at us. That's how Velcro was invented. A thistle got stuck in a hiker's sock. The hiker, George de Mestral, wondered how something could penetrate both his sock and his dog's fur so easily and still be so difficult to remove. He also wondered if it could be useful for something. Though it took him a decade to succeed, he kept using his creative imagination to invent one of the most useful tools of the twentieth century.[4]

Creative expression through play, the arts, scientific discovery, technology, innovation, and invention enhances our resilience because it enables us to express our inexpressible inner self in a way that we can see as well as integrate what we couldn't express in thought or word. We don't have to be "an artist" to benefit from

---

3. G.S. Cohen, GD, *The Creative Age: Awakening Human Potential in the Second Half of Life*. (New York, NY: Harper Collins, 2000), 13.
4. "George de Mestral: Velcro Inventor." Smithsonian Institute Lemelson Center for the Study of Invention and Innovation. April 15, 2014. http://invention.si.edu/george-de-mestral-velcro-inventor.

this aspect of creativity. We can simply be someone who is playing around with color, or movement, or sound, or words, or any other medium that captures our imagination and engages us in doing something with it. "Wherever the soul is in need," writes Shaun McNiff, "art presents itself as a resourceful helper."[5]

The apostle Paul said we are God's creative expression (*poiema*) in the world, created in Christ to do great things (Ephesians 2:10). The Greek word is the root of our word poem. A poet plays with words and how they sit on the page, making use of word order, punctuation, and space in ways that ignore the rules of language we think we have to follow so that we can see more than we could before.

> Elizabeth Barrett Browning wrote,
>
> "Earth's crammed with heaven,
>
> And every common bush afire with God,
>
> But only he who sees takes off his shoes;
>
> The rest sit round and pluck blackberries."

In times of grief and difficulty, our vision and our vocabulary have a tendency to shrink. Offering one another the space to play with our words and repunctuate our presence are gifts of resilience that create the chance to see what lies beyond the seemingly insurmountable obstacle.

---

5. S. McNiff, *Art Heals: How Creativity Cures the Soul* (flyleaf). (Boston, MA: Shambhala, 2004).

4 ▪ Looking for Strengths

David Cooperrider, the founder of Appreciative Inquiry, points to the importance of looking for strength in the system.[6] As a business consultant, he was often flying into different cities, being met at the airport by a representative of the entity with whom he was called to work. On the way from airport to hotel, he reported, he often heard engaging stories about the company; energy and enthusiasm were high. When the group gathered in corporate headquarters at breakfast the next morning, the dynamics had changed. As the problems facing the institution were listed, spirits dragged; energy rapidly disappeared. His awareness of this phenomenon was instrumental in the formulation of the process known as Appreciative Inquiry. A similar shift can happen when that approach is applied to leadership within a system. A parish had been struggling for several years, apparently stuck in some sort of rut, with negativity bouncing from one place within the structure to another. As soon as toxic personalities rotated off the vestry, another would pop up in the Episcopal Church Women (ECW) or the altar guild or choir.

---

6. David Cooperrider and Suresh Srivastva of Case Western Reserve University are credited with being the "parents" of a process whose thesis is that an organization can be recreated by its conversations, or story-telling, in a life-giving way when the conversations are shaped by appreciative questions that allow the identification of what is valued in the life of the organization.

"We seem to always be dealing with negative personalities," the rector sighed.

"What might happen if, instead of focusing on the negative, you looked for pockets of strength or potential for strength?" a parish consultant suggested.

"But these people are pretty powerful," the rector said.

"There is power in strength, whether it carries a title or not," the consultant observed. "Let's look at the parish list, and see where you think there might be untapped potential." He encouraged the rector to think of characteristics that might represent strengths—fresh eyes and insight; more responsive than reactive; firm in their values and beliefs without being polarized; able to think reflectively; self-aware. After a list had been developed, individuals were invited to attend the first of a series of educational sessions about effective leadership behaviors.

The first place to notice change was the Episcopal Church Women (ECW). A struggle had been simmering over old hurts, complete with parking lot conversations, divisive e-mails gone viral, and newer members staying away from the unpleasant tensions.

Pat, who had attended the training session for leaders, was approached after one ECW meeting by Gail, who wanted to complain about Susie. That's triangulation, Pat thought to herself.

"You need to talk to Susie about your concerns," she said.

"Oh, I couldn't do that," Gail responded. "I might hurt her feelings, and I know she doesn't mean anything bad. But you could. . . ."

"No," Pat said firmly. "You need to go to her directly and tell her that when such-and-such happens, it makes you feel a certain way."

Gail continued to protest, asking Pat to do the work for her.

"You need to talk with her directly," Pat maintained. "If you are uncomfortable doing it alone, I will go with you. But you need to set it up."

The appointment was made, and after a bit of coaching on Pat's part, the two met with Susie. Gail was uncertain—the bravado of the parking lot dissipating face-to-face with her nemesis. Pat's presence provided a reassurance.

"Susie, when you made a choice to invite some members of our ECW to go with you to the museum on the same day my psychologist daughter-in-law was speaking about "What Is a Family?" and told people that you didn't need to hear that liberal stuff because you know what a real family is, I felt really hurt personally, and I felt bad for my daughter-in-law that someone I consider a friend was not only attempting to pull members away from a guest speaker's program, but also disparaging her professional expertise." Gail's voice had picked up volume and strength as she spoke, and now she paused for a breath.

Susie looked down at the floor, and then at Gail. "I wasn't thinking about your daughter-in-law or you," she said in a strained voice. "I just hate hearing all of these things that go against everything I've been taught or believed all of my life. It's scary!"

"I wish you had said that to me and to the group when we planned the program," Gail said. "There might be other people who felt that way and my daughter-in-law could have planned a discussion around it."

They had initiated a new process.

The process was taken a step further when the rector recognized that there were both subtle and not-so-subtle bullying tactics keeping the vestry stuck during its meetings. Some of the bullying was passive-aggressive and more easily spotted. The less easily recognized bullying came in the form of aggrandizing behavior that intimidated others; rather than speaking out in meetings, they took their concerns into postmeeting e-mails and parking lot conversations. The "bullying" took the form of impressive-sounding opinions, often backed by professional articles (little of which might actually be relevant to the subject at hand) and references to conversations with influential people in the community and diocese. These were often accompanied by nonverbal gestures of impatience when clarifying questions were asked, as if to say "Any dummy would know that!"

The more aggressive bullying came in blatant attempts by the senior warden to railroad items in meetings: going around the rector, attempting to take the chair without being asked to do so, withholding information, openly criticizing, staying away from meetings.

A bishop discovered a practice in his new diocese of giving annual $10,000 grants to a list of parishes that were "barely making it." Early in his tenure, the bishop announced that he was cutting off those grants and opening the grant application process to anyone who was interested. The parishes that had their funding cut believed that it was the worst thing that had ever happened to them.

Two years after the change in granting procedures, one of the parishes asked to speak to the annual diocesan convention. "What we thought was the worst thing that ever happened to us turned out to be the best thing," the deputies said. "It was the only way we would ever have grown up. We were on life support. To continue on that path would have broken us completely, and broken the system down. We were told to go do it—and we did. And we're stronger than ever today."

5 ▪ Fostering Compassion

Outside the church doors, there was nothing even remotely civil about the most recent political campaigns. Plural. From local runs for mayor or county official to the nation's highest office, name calling, truth stretching, denigrating the "other" and what they aren't rather than establishing what one *is* . . . the ugliness flowed across the nation via TV screens, social media, and newspapers—a stream of toxic negativity that pushed polarization to unprecedented heights. We've also heard painful stories of athletic abuse finally called by its proper name—child sexual abuse—and the pretense of being individuals above suspicion that allowed that abuse. As athletic temples cleanse their rolls of those who don't win enough, rabid fans scream, "I don't care what else he's done, so long as he wins!" The fan in the stands with the loudest voice just might be bringing the same "win at all costs" attitude to the vestry table.

Far from being countercultural and behaving in ways that are congruent with the life and teaching of Jesus Christ, we have brought the hostile, the polarizing, the toxic with us into our naves and parish halls. There are those who cry loudly about the effect the culture has on the church. This is not about modern culture seeping into naves and parish halls, puffs of smoke under doorways and through vents and windows like poison gas, but about unholy behaviors marching with us right into our pews, becoming acceptable parts of the very fabric of our lives.

"We've gone beyond corporate-think and corporate-speak and into 'Survivor' mentality," a man said. "Who are we going to vote off of the island?" American Public Media's Krista Tippett offered a series on the most polarizing issues in our country on her syndicated program, "On Being." Former archenemies Jonathan Rauch and David Blankenhorn battled mightily and publicly over protection of heterosexual marriage and advocacy of gay marriage before becoming friends and collaborators. "There's nothing soft and squishy about that," said one. "There's something higher than being right."

It is also hard work. The acceptance of that reality—that being the difference, making the change is hard, hard work—is a moment when a truth is named and taken inside the heart, mind, and spirit in a way that changes everything. The "ah-ha" moment that recognizes the difficulty of the task precedes the determination to *be* the change you want to see in the world. In her book *Turning to One Another: Simple Conversations to Restore Hope to the Future*, Margaret Wheatley shares a story from the Aztec people of Mexico:

> It is said by our grandparents that a long time ago there was a great fire in the forests that covered our Earth. People and animals started to run, trying to escape from the fire. Our brother owl, Tecoloti, was running away also

when he noticed a small bird hurrying back and forth between the nearest river and the fire. He headed toward this small bird.

He noticed that it was our brother the Quetzal bird, running to the river, picking up small drops of water in his beak, then returning to the fire to throw that tiny bit of water on the flame. Owl approached Quetzal bird and yelled at him: "What are you doing brother? Are you stupid? You are not going to achieve anything by doing this. What are you trying to do? You must run for your life!"

Quetzal bird stopped for a moment and looked at owl, and then answered: "I am doing the best I can with what I have."

It is remembered by our Grandparents that a long time ago the forests that covered our Earth were saved from a great fire by a small Quetzal bird, an owl, and many other animals and people who got together and put out the flame.[7]

It happened on the road to Emmaus. It is the grace of transfiguration. In this post-Christian time in our church, it continues to happen.

---

7. Margaret Wheatley, *Turning to One Another: Conversations to Restore Hope to the Future* (San Francisco: Berrett-Koehler, 2002), 126–127.

A priest, part of a diocesan leadership team, was in a small rural parish. It was the second week of a three-week series, and the "Holy Conversations" had moved from stories of times they had been most engaged in their parishes to times they had been hurt and disappointed. For many years, this small group of faithful people had lived in the fear that someday, for some reason, their church might simply disappear and with it, the opportunity for an alternative to the fundamentalism in their area. At times, the tension brought anxieties that threatened to destroy them from within. In these brave and honest conversations, they were naming the behaviors that had held them hostage, determining to take specific steps to not just survive, but do mission and ministry in their community. Above all, they were determined not to allow the return of the destructive behaviors that were the true threat to their survival.

"As I listened," the priest said, "I was overwhelmed with emotion at their faithfulness, and at the importance of what they, and we, are doing. I am aware that these things require time, as well as psychological, spiritual, and emotional energy, and that sometimes it's just easier to follow some program from somewhere than it is to build healthy relationships. We have lots of metrics for measuring efficiency and what we call effectiveness. We don't have metrics for faithfulness and wholeness. And I was so thankful that I am a part of something where we're not taking the easy route— for this work deserves all of the support that we can give it."

The good news is that all of us have the opportunity to be the Quetzal bird, or one who joins the Quetzal's brigade. The additional news is that we must continue hurrying back and forth with the water, for the fire is large and spreading rapidly. We will grow weary and want to quit. Putting out the fires of damaging behaviors requires endless repetitions, time, and psychological, emotional, and spiritual energy.

Shinichi Suzuki, the Japanese violin pedagogue, tells his students that in order to incorporate a change in their playing, the new way must be repeated at least one hundred times in succession. If the old way intervenes, the count begins again.

Repetition, repetition, repetition.

Change *is* hard. But the cost of not changing is unthinkable. And the gift you pass on to your part of the world could be good patterns of functional behaviors, congruent with the life and teachings of Jesus, patterns that free us to respond fully to our charge to bring the Kingdom of God to earth here and now.

Pockets of this Kingdom work exist today: local efforts spotted across the face of the Church. History reminds us that when local efforts become connected, amazing things can happen. As long as those efforts exist in isolation, nothing will change. But the connection of local simultaneous actions can result in something much more powerful than the sum of their parts. As the transformation comes, we must hold it high and sing its song, so that others will see and know that it is real and here to stay.

We are presently in a between-time—on a bridge between where we have been and where we must go. The way ahead is not clear, which makes it difficult to step out in faith. Like Abraham and Sarah, if we choose to answer the call that means new life, we will leave much behind. One of the things that we will leave behind is the need to know now. And with us, we will take the awareness that we are embracing a new and foundational call that must continue with us, beyond our time, perhaps forever. It is hard to imagine a time when living and working together would not be a priority.

True leadership is generative. It provides replicable models, not rigid prescriptions to be mimicked without thought or integration. This kind of life-giving leadership, at all levels of our life together, is within our grasp, as we choose to walk into the light of God's new heaven and earth.

The poet David Whyte, in the afterword of his book *Leading from Within: Poetry That Sustains the Courage to Lead*, references those who are "students of leadership."

> Students of leadership, are, I believe, of all ages, all descriptions of humanity. I hope to always be one. I invite you to be one, too—enabling the change you want to see in the world. Some of you will speak with words that the leaders of today do not know, for they do not yet exist.

You will create ways we cannot imagine for situations unknown to those of us alive today. If the church and the world are to survive, the concept you will make your own is this one thing: we must find a way to live and work together.[8]

---

8. David Whyte, in "Afterword," *Leading from Within* (San Francisco, CA: Jossey-Bass, 2009), 239.

6 ▪ Giving Up Control

Mother Cecily Broderick y Guerra was the first female rector of St. Philip's Episcopal Church in Harlem in the early 2000s. She preached a gospel of transformation and stirring up a congregation comprised largely of financially comfortable middle-aged and senior African Americans.

"You need to test yourself, see whether you're holding onto something the Spirit leads you to or if you're clinging to something because you can't imagine life any other way," she warned the congregation as she strolled the center aisle, preaching without text and looking into parishioners' eyes with a mix of urgency, patience, humor, and hope. "So watch out, because staying blind and hard-hearted can be an obstacle to your own discipleship."

She later reflected, "A lot of people here aren't open to what the Spirit is dictating. They view the future by walking backward, and they have no tolerance for change. So I continue to reflect in my preaching that change is a part of life. It's not a reflection of failure. It's a reflection of being alive."

That's a tough gospel to live by. God knows we want to cling to something tangible, to stick with the way things have always been, to maintain traditional boundaries regarding who's in and who's out. But faith and real life come when we cling not to our own power or ability or institutions, but only to the living God. And sometimes the greatest blessing is that which wrenches our fingers off the controls and removes the illusion that we were ever in charge.

God has been calling humanity to risk and surrender like this for ages. We have already heard the bold witness of prophets like Isaiah, who shared God's plan to make all things new and God's hope that we would join that holy venture. Everywhere Jesus went, he held out his hand and said, "Drop your nets and follow me." He invited people into a life of abandon, a life of deep awareness and presence, a life transgressing the boundaries the world constructs, and all in order to get to God.

Jesus continues to ask us, "Do you think you know who's inside and holy, or who is outside and unclean? Are you sure what is pure? Are you certain death is the end? Ah, think again." He crossed lines and defied limits throughout his life—and beyond—to convince us that we could let go of our assumptions, expectations, and so-called knowledge, surrender and rest in God, who alone has the final word.

Surrendering to God—relinquishing control—is not a benign act. Maybe that is because God is not a benign God. In a pastoral letter dated June 23, 2004, the Episcopal Church's then-Presiding Bishop, Frank Griswold, asked members torn by disagreement and misunderstanding to trust and not be "undone by God's wild and unpredictable ways." He continued:

> The love of Christ, given root-room within us, is a danger-
> ous force. We know that—as was the case for St. Peter—
> love can take us where we do not wish to go. It can require
> us to die to our desire for safety. It can demand a

relinquishment of our carefully crafted plans, of our fondly held views, and of our clear expectations.[9]

So much of our time in church is spent maintaining and protecting: buildings, doctrines, traditions, plans, expectations. God does not change, and the church—as God's people on earth—is not supposed to change.

But what if that is not our call at all? What if, as Griswold suggests, the love of Christ is actually supposed to free us, to make us imaginative and resilient and fearless enough to go wherever the God of transformation would have us go? What if closing the door to change, something we might have done out of love for our traditions and communities, actually closes the door to the Spirit of God?

Benedictine nun and Catholic theologian Joan Chittister warns that church folk too often tip in that very direction:

> To close ourselves off from the wisdom of the world around us in the name of God is a kind of spiritual arrogance exceeded by little else in the human lexicon of errors. It makes of life a kind of prison where, in the name of

---

9. The Most Reverend Frank Griswold, "A Word to the Church from the Presiding Bishop," June 23, 2004 (Episcopal News Service, www.episcopalchurch.org/3577_41633_ENG_HTM.htm). See Acts 8.

holiness, thought is chained and vision is condemned. It makes us our own gods. It is a sorry excuse for spirituality. The implications of that kind of closing out the multiple revelations of the mind of God are weighty: once we shut our hearts to the other, we have shut our hearts to God.[10]

Chittister claims there is a spiritual discipline in the act of maintaining a posture of utter receptivity and hospitality to new voices, new people, new ideas, new music, new words, new power. By opening our minds, our hearts, our very selves to The Other—the person of a different culture or ethnicity, the person of a different generation, the person of a different class background, the person of a different sexual orientation—we are letting go of our idols and practicing for that greater opening, the complete opening to the God who wants to be all in all *in us*. Being open, discerning God's presence in surprising places, is an act of love, surrender, and faith like no other.

---

10. Joan Chittister, *Illuminated Life: Monastic Wisdom for Seekers of Light* (Maryknoll, NY: Orbis Books, 2000), 88.

7 ▪ Be Not Afraid

Fear assails us all in so many forms it can seem unmanageable, but the Bible's response to fear is clear and unwavering: be not afraid.

- Isaiah heard that message, and as a result he wrote: "Surely God is my salvation; I will trust and will not be afraid, for the Lord God is my strength and my might; he has become my salvation" (Isaiah 12:2).
- The Psalmist heard it, and that faith inspired this song: "God is our refuge and strength, a very present help in trouble. Therefore we will not fear, though the earth should change, though the mountains shake in the heart of the sea; though its waters roar and foam, though the mountains tremble with its tumult" (Psalm 46:1–3).
- Jesus spoke these words as he prepared the disciples for his coming death: "Peace I leave with you; my peace I give to you. I do not give to you as the world gives. Do not let your hearts be troubled, and do not let them be afraid" (John 14:27).

Be not afraid. When the words or the message appear in scripture, they usually herald some dramatic shift just around the bend. God's people are predictably confused, tempted to hide their heads and pray for the tempest to pass. Then God speaks a word—"Be not afraid"—and beckons them to continue on the path, and the story of faith lives on.

Alas, when we hear "Be not afraid," the gut response may be to assume fear is the enemy, a demon to be exorcised. Western culture trains us to run from our fear and other "dark emotions" like despair and grief. "The fear of falling into the darkness, of going down and not being able to come up, lurks right at the edge of our ability to feel at all," Greenspan explains. "Our culture reinforces this fear, which I call 'emotion-phobia.'"[11] We Christians make life harder still whenever we shove fear down while declaring that the opposite of faith is not doubt but fear. If we confess fear or anxiety, somehow that sounds like an admission that we lack the strong faith and backbone of more mature believers. So, we cover it like the dreaded scarlet letter that marks us as weak believers or bad people.

Especially when the fear or resistance surfaces while we are engaged in doing noble, Christian work, it can seem nearly impossible to admit our discomfort. At the Cathedral Church of St. Paul in Boston, Massachusetts, homeless and poor people are leaders throughout the parish and have claimed the church as their own. It is a fulfillment of the gospel vision. It also means many economically privileged people approach looking for *their* Episcopal Church, only to turn away from the throng of unwashed masses who know this church as a sanctuary.

---

11. Miriam Greenspan, *Healing Through the Dark Emotions: The Wisdom of Grief, Fear and Despair* (Boston: Shambhala Publications, 2003), 169–70.

When Stephanie Spellers served at St. Paul, she recalled speaking with colleagues at a nearby church that didn't open its doors so widely, saying they looked at her with pity: "Oh, you're the ones with all the homeless people." Were there limits to radical welcome, she wondered, especially if it was creating this kind of press and causing others to find us somehow unwelcoming? What were the real costs of maintaining this gospel-based identity? Did she secretly fear being further marginalized by our association with the homeless?

Of course, liberal Christians want to see ourselves as those who welcome *all* people at God's table! Of course, we are willing to make *some* changes in order to welcome them. We congratulate ourselves for being so much warmer and friendlier than some other group or congregation. We say we do not feel awkward or anxious in the presence of someone who is oppressed and does not have the privilege and access we take for granted. We tell ourselves we would be overjoyed and pleased to have "them" as part of our congregations (and declare it a shame that they do not seem to want to join us). No one wants to be a racist, a homophobe, or a snob. No one wants to seem inhospitable in our polite church culture.

Meanwhile, we ignore the frisson of anxiety and the voice that whispers, "I don't know how to do this. I don't want to do this. Why are we going through this? God, why do things keep changing?" We keep silent, shove the fear down, pray for freedom from this sin. In one workshop, a woman admitted her desire to take scissors to her fear and "cut it all out." We want to clear out the evidence of our weakness, to deal quickly and move on, to use our rational minds and make sense of these nonsensical impulses. Then, we have been told, we will be free.

Except that the promised freedom doesn't actually materialize. Cut, and you only slice away at yourself. Rationalize, and the feelings remain. Deny, and the truth pops up in another place. If you have ever tried any of these tactics, and at some point all of us have, then you know they bring little more than short-term relief, if that. Why? Because, as Elizabeth Lesser tells it, "Repressed pain never goes away. It is stored in the heart, in the body, and even in the genes."[12] Repression, denial, and silence are not the same as healing. The way of genuine transformation and wholeness—the real invitation behind the admonition to "Be not afraid"—travels a different route.

Buddhist teacher Machik Labdrön points the way with this refreshing insight: "In other traditions, demons are expelled externally. But in my tradition demons are accepted with compassion."[13] The "demon" of fear is not some external force. It is part of human nature, and thus part of our own makeup. What a gift it would

---

12. Elizabeth Lesser, *Broken Open: How Difficult Times Can Help Us Grow* (New York: Villard Books, 2004), 62.
13. As quoted in Pema Chodrön, *The Places that Scare You: A Guide to Fearlessness in Difficult Times* (Boston: Shambala Publications, 2002), 49.

be to learn finally to love what American Buddhist leader Pema Chodrön calls that "shaky and tender place," the place deep inside that holds our fear of The Other, our fear of change, and our fear of loss:

> Tapping into that shaky and tender place has a transformative effect. Being in this place may feel uncertain and edgy, but it's also a big relief. Just to stay there, even for a moment, feels like a genuine act of kindness to ourselves. Being compassionate enough to accommodate our own fears takes courage, of course, and it definitely feels counterintuitive. But it's what we need to do.[14]

Sitting in this way may at first seem self-indulgent and terribly nonproductive. Then we begin to shudder and feel "uncertain and edgy." Difficult as it is, we have no choice but to approach the demon with care and kindness. If we do, Chodrön promises, the effect will be transformative. I believe that is because sitting with fear nurtures within us three spiritual gifts: wisdom, freedom, and faith.

---

14. Chodrön, *The Places That Scare You*, 49.

8 ▪ Fear and Wisdom

Fear is a wise teacher, and shoving it aside without listening actually places us in more danger, not less. As Miguel de Cervantes wisely noted: "Fear is sharp-sighted, and can see things underground."[15] If we fear walking around an unfamiliar neighborhood at night, it may be because we are unsure of our surroundings. That fear is smart, and should lead us to walk with a companion. The pandemic has called for an informed fear that takes seriously the need to wear masks, wash our hands, and keep our physical distance. To ignore that fear is to risk our lives and the lives of those around us. Telling the truth about fear, no matter how ugly or vulnerable it makes us feel, is the beginning of wisdom.

15. As quoted in Greenspan, *Healing Through the Dark Emotions*, 169.

9 ▪ Fear and Freedom

Facing fear can also make us free. Much of the journey of life requires facing our own stifling, confining fears: the personal, interpersonal, institutional, and cultural ones. Beginning to walk toward those fears and toward the loss and pain that lurk in the corner of all fear is the difference between walking into the wind backward and suddenly realizing that if you only step forward, the wind will be at your back and you could run. Or, as Elizabeth Lesser puts it,

> We live in a river of change, and a river of change lives within us. Every day we're given a choice: We can relax and float in the direction that the water flows, or we can swim hard against it. If we go with the river, the energy of a thousand mountain streams will be with us, filling our hearts with courage and enthusiasm. If we resist the river, we will feel rankled and tired as we tread water, stuck in the same place.[16]

Denying pain and fear only shackles and weakens us. We can lean into 1 John 4:18:

> There is no fear in love, but perfect love casts out fear; for fear has to do with punishment, and whoever fears has not reached perfection in love.

---

16. Lesser, *Broken Open*, 237.

The Greek word rendered as "perfect" might be better understood as "fully realized"—the kind of love that knows how to survive difficult vestry meetings and long-standing traditions, remote worship and the loss of fellowship; the kind of love that knows fear is never the last word.

10 ▪ Fear and Faith

When we stop running away from fear, we can experience true vulnerability, the sort that is only possible when you finally stand in the storm, lift your hands in surrender, and pray that all is not lost. That is when God loves to step in: when we are at our most confused, our most desperate, our most needy. Like the disciples on a storm-tossed sea, we may grow frightened and fear the end is near. But Jesus walks out to join us with these words, "It is I; do not be afraid" (John 6:16–21; Matthew 14:22–27). Do not be paralyzed by your fear. Do not be consumed with anger. Do not get stuck on the defensive. Do not run from The Other. Our fear of change and pain is powerful and frightening, but Jesus waits to offer us healing and renewal, imploring us to keep on moving, promising we may be tossed and even broken, but we will not be overcome.

In her book *Traveling Mercies*, Anne Lamott shares her own experience with being broken open by pain. She found herself floundering following the death of her best friend in the world and the end of a romantic relationship. Finally, in a passage I discovered soon after my father's death, she writes of what I now understand to be the grace of grieving and sitting with pain:

> The depth of feeling continued to surprise and threaten me, but each time it hit again and I bore it, like a nicotine craving, I would discover that it hadn't washed me away. After a while it was like an inside shower, washing off some

of the rust and calcification in my pipes. It was like giving a dry garden a good watering. Don't get me wrong: grief sucks; it really does. Unfortunately, though, avoiding it robs us of life, of the now, of a sense of living spirit. Mostly I have tried to avoid it by staying very busy, working too hard, trying to achieve as much as possible. But the bad news is that whatever you use to keep the pain at bay robs you of the flecks and nuggets of gold that feeling grief will give you. A fixation can keep you nicely defined and give you the illusion that your life has not fallen apart. But since your life may have indeed fallen apart, the illusion won't hold up forever, and if you are lucky and brave, you will be willing to bear disillusion. You begin to cry and writhe and yell and then to keep on crying; and then, finally, grief ends up giving you the two best things: softness and illumination.[17]

Lamott's situation did not drastically improve when she began to face her own demons. However, our ability to keep walking with courage, hope, wisdom, and compassion is incalculably greater when there is room for God to enter and offer us those two best things: softness and illumination. God does not actively send us trials to test us or push us into deeper faith. That said, we can rest assured that God delights when we turn, softened and broken hearts in hand, and beg God to be our companion in the way.

---

17. Anne Lamott, *Traveling Mercies* (New York: Anchor, 2000), 72.

11 ▪ Practicing Resurrection

Fear is never the final word in any story with God. Far more often, the bold act of acknowledging fear starts a new chapter. For Christians, that is the whole story of the Resurrection. We are invited to participate in Christ's death and in his resurrection, to let the power that destroyed death now free us to be the living body of Christ. Many churches attempt to bring this theology alive by placing the baptismal font near the entry, where members must walk by it to come inside. On the one hand, this move signifies that baptism is our entry into the household of Christ. But at a deeper level, we are reminded that we have been literally baptized into the entire life, death, and resurrection of Christ. We are members of his body, and if it has been raised, then we will be raised, as well.

Resurrection does not simply come on some unknown but imagined day when God will raise all those who have lived in God's embrace. It is a resurrection we can experience whenever we face death—all the tiny deaths that threaten to sap our souls. It is a resurrection that allows us to occupy a completely new posture in our daily lives. If death is not the end, if God's power defeats any enemy, including the most fearsome of all, then we can step forward and proclaim, hope, serve, and love without fear. Rainer Maria Rilke shares this stirring promise in one of his *Love Poems to God*:

> God speaks to each of us as he makes us
>
> then walks with us silently out of the night.
>
> These are the words we dimly hear:

You, sent out beyond your recall,

go to the limits of your longing.

Embody me.

Flare up like flame

and make big shadows I can move in.

Let everything happen to you: beauty and terror.

Just keep going. No feeling is final.

Don't let yourself lose me.

Nearby is the country they call Life.

You will know it by its seriousness.

Give me your hand.[18]

Taking on the voice of God, Rilke urges his reader to engage everything life has to offer—its beauty and its terror, the changes and the losses, the joy and the pain—knowing that no feeling lasts forever. The pain will come, but surely it will reveal something of God to us. The grain of wheat will fall into the ground and die, but that is the only way for it to bear fruit. If we are not looking

---

18. Rainer Maria Rilke, *Rilke's Book of Hours: Love Poems to God*
    (No. I.59), translated by Anita Barrows and Joanna Macy
    (New York: Riverhead, 1996), 88.

back at mistakes and pains or ahead for trouble and loss, then we find ourselves in a glorious, hopeful present moment, and that is precisely where the God of life waits to take our hand.

If we know ourselves to be unconditionally loved like that, if we know even death is not the end, Henri Nouwen points out that we are dangerously free to love and surrender all for Christ.[19] We can go anywhere, even if it means we might be rejected, even if it means we have to look deep into the heart of our own fear. We can go to the most terrifying place in the world, because we know we are "loved beyond [the] boundaries" of the world.

Let us listen for these words when we imagine we are stepping into that place of terror, uncertainty, chaos, and fear; remember them as we take that step: *Be not afraid.* You are loved. *Be not afraid.* You are held. *Be not afraid.* You are God's own. *Be not afraid.* We will face our fear and we will live. *Be not afraid.* We have been called to live as the children of a radically welcoming God. Let us allow our very hearts and minds to be broken open to make room for The Other *and* for God. *Be not afraid.*

The hope of the Resurrection is that life lies beyond the grave, beyond our fears, beyond our failures, even beyond our sins. Hope is stronger than thinking things will get better. It is, we might say, realistic optimism—which clarifies the difference between optimism and wishful thinking. Wishful thinking—the belief that something we want to have happen will happen, even though that's

---

19. Robert A. Jonas, ed., *Henri Nouwen: Writings Selected* (Maryknoll, NY: Orbis Books, 1998), 72.

not likely or possible—is an obstacle to resilience. Wishful thinking that isn't intercepted and replaced by a realistic perspective can lead to delays, poor decisions, disillusionment, heartbreak, and despair. In contrast, realistic optimism is a combination of optimism—thinking from a positive perspective—and pessimism—thinking from a negative perspective. The mix of optimism and pessimism minimizes the disadvantages of being overly optimistic by including an assessment from the negative side of the situation. Yet at the same time, the energy that's generated by seeing the positive side helps to overcome the discouragement engendered by the negative assessment.[20] When we engage both optimism and pessimism in our response to adversity, we're building realistic optimism. It's a powerful resilience skill because we're engaging opposite traits at the same time—a known factor in the capacity to adapt to new conditions.[21]

Hope adds action to realistic optimism. Snyder found that hope actually engages us in action. C. R. Snyder, a pioneer in the study of hope, found that in addition to having the quality of a positive attitude, hope has three other elements: setting a goal we want to attain, envisioning possible ways to reach that goal, and taking specific steps along one or more of those ways toward attaining

---

20. A. Siebert, *The Resiliency Advantage: Master Change, Thrive under Pressure, and Bounce Back from Setbacks.* (San Francisco, CA: Berrett-Koehler, 2005).
21. Siebert, *The Resiliency Advantage: Master Change, Thrive under Pressure, and Bounce Back from Setbacks,* 25–37.

our goal.[22] This process can take a while. Then, it works well to keep a long-range goal in mind but also to plan a series of short-term goals that we can accomplish one at a time. As we experience the satisfaction of reaching our smaller goals, we'll either be able to see the possibility of reaching our long-range goal or we may see that an alternative goal would be better. In either case, hope and realistic optimism help us meet adverse challenges with resilience. They engage us in taking stock of our situation, setting short-term and long-term goals, planning small steps we can take toward attaining these goals, and taking those steps as soon as we're able.

---

22. C.R. Snyder, *The Psychology of Hope: You Can Get There from Here* (New York, NY: The Free Press, 1994).

A Final Thought

Walk on to the Green of any little New England town, and you will find century-old trees offering shade in the summer and flaming radiance in the fall. They stand tall, even majestic, and yet they are full of wounds and imperfections—a twisted branch, a deeply scarred bark, a knothole or two—each one a sign of the tree's resilience. And each of the wounds tells a story of a storm, a bicycle crash, or the mark of someone's pocket knife.

Walk into most any congregation, and the dynamic is much the same: how they have lived through the hopes and fears of all the years shows through in how they have grown and how they have failed to move beyond certain traumas. Any congregation that still functions is a picture of resilience.

Much has been made in recent years of the decline in membership in mainline churches and seminaries. The pandemic has hastened the closing of some parishes that might otherwise have hung on for a few more years. The story of the Church feels different from the oak on the Green in that the tree keeps growing; we are getting smaller. Then again, size and growth may not be quite the synonyms we think they are at times. A congregation that grows in compassion, courage, and creativity may be healthier and even more hopeful than one set on simply packing the pews.

Measuring growth begins with a sense of who we are right now. We have to start with the ecclesiastical equivalent of the dated pencil mark on the door frame that shows how tall we stood at that moment. Like Joshua telling the Hebrew people to stack up the stones so they could remember who they were and tell the stories, we have to be intentional about returning to the marks that have defined us and to remind ourselves who we have been and who we are.

The Mother Church of Christian Science in Boston has a ring of skylights in the dome of the sanctuary. Because of the fear that Hitler was going to bomb the East Coast during World War II, the skylights were painted over. And forgotten. In the early nineties a renovation crew removed the paint and brought fresh light to the room a half a century later. Between the time the skylights were painted and then uncovered, the congregation had met for worship in that room most every week, but they forgot to keep telling the story.

Who a congregation can become depends a good bit on who they think they are and how well they tell stories of who they have been. To tell our stories well is to understand that, at least in some ways, they are grief stories. The stories of our lives are stories of loss and how we lived with and through those losses. And they keep piling up. As a Resurrection people we know loss is not the period on the sentence. We also know, like the old tree, we can grow strong at the broken places.

Love is stronger than death. Love is stronger than committee meetings. Love will give us the resilience to grow together.

CPSIA information can be obtained
at www.ICGtesting.com
Printed in the USA
FSHW021814010521
80928FS